JIM JACKSON

ROLANDO BLACKMAN

DIRK NOWITZKI

DEREK HARPER

SAM PERKINS

JAMES DONALDSON

JASON KIDD

ROY TARPLEY

STEVE NASH

BRAD DAVIS

MICHAEL FINLEY

MARK AGUIRRE

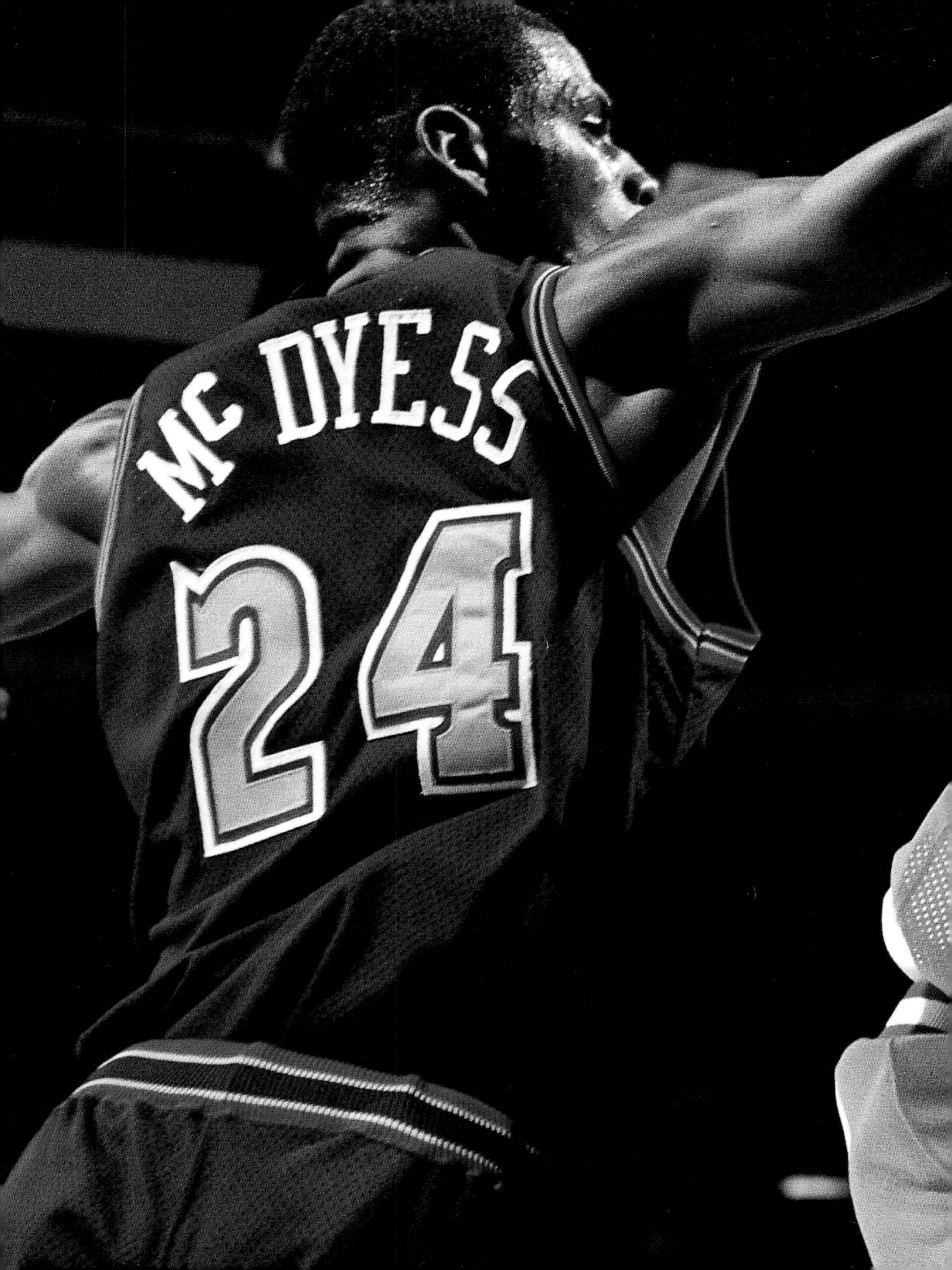
McDYESS
24

CREATIVE C EDUCATION

AARON FRISCH

Published by Creative Education, 123 South Broad Street, Mankato, MN 56001

Creative Education is an imprint of The Creative Company.

Designed by Rita Marshall

Photos by Allsport, Rich Kane, NBA Photos, SportsChrome

Library of Congress Cataloging-in-Publication Data

Frisch, Aaron. The history of the Dallas Mavericks / by Aaron Frisch.

p. cm. – (Pro basketball today)   ISBN 1-58341-095-3

1. Dallas Mavericks (Basketball team)–History–

Juvenile literature. [1. Dallas Mavericks (Basketball team)–History.

2. Basketball–History.] I. Title. II. Series.

GV885.52.D34 F75 2001   796.323'64'097642812–dc21   00-047343

First Edition 9 8 7 6 5 4 3 2 1

DALLAS
IS A LARGE CITY
LOCATED ON THE ROLLING
PRAIRIE OF NORTHERN TEXAS. TODAY KNOWN AS

"Big D," Dallas started out as a lonely frontier town. A trader named

John Neely Bryan founded the settlement in 1841 and soon named it

after George M. Dallas, the vice president of the United States in the

late 1840s. As the city grew, it became a major center for banking and

cotton production.

Ranching was also big business on the prairie surrounding Dallas.

In the 1800s, cowboys often drove huge herds of horses or cattle across

the vast Texas landscape. Common among these herds were mavericks—

BRAD DAVIS

wild, headstrong animals that refused to stay with the rest of the herd.

Today, Dallas is also the home of a professional basketball team named

"Mavericks" was
selected over
"Wranglers"
and "Express"
as the name
of Dallas's
NBA franchise
in **1980**.
the Mavericks, which joined the National Basketball

Association (NBA) in 1980.

{THE FIRST MAVS} The Mavericks were optimistic

heading into their first season. Their head coach was Dick

Motta, who just two years earlier had led the Washington

6   Bullets to the NBA championship. Motta was known as a demanding

leader who got the most out of his players.

Most of Coach Motta's lineup consisted of little-known players

who had been cut from other teams. One player who made a strong

impression around the league, though, was point guard Brad Davis, who

emerged as a team leader and a sure ball handler. Still, the Mavericks

went only 15–67 that first season.

MICHAEL FINLEY

Rolando Blackman averaged 19 points a game over his 11 years in Dallas.

ROLANDO BLACKMAN

Dallas then selected three talented rookies in the 1981 NBA Draft: guard Rolando Blackman and forwards Mark Aguirre and Jay Vincent. Aguirre and Vincent gave the team plenty of muscle, while Blackman proved to be a fierce defender and a great outside shooter. "Rolando Blackman might be the cleverest guard in the NBA," said broadcaster Chuck Daly. "He's a great clutch player. . . ."

In **1982–83**, forward Pat Cummings became the first Mavs player with a 20-rebound game.

These young stars combined to go 28–54 in 1981–82, nearly doubling their win total from the previous season. Two years later, the Mavericks made the playoffs for the first time. The main reason for their success was Aguirre. With a deadly shooting touch and an assortment of spinning low-post moves, the powerful forward seemed unstoppable. Aguirre finished second in the NBA in scoring with nearly 30 points per game and became Dallas's first All-Star.

9

PAT CUMMINGS

Guard Derek Harper led the Mavericks in assists for seven seasons in a row.

DEREK HARPER

{MOVING UP IN "BIG D"} In 1983 and 1984, the Mavericks

continued to have great success in the NBA Draft, picking up guard

The Mavericks were the best three-point shooting team in the NBA in **1985–86**.

Derek Harper and forward Sam Perkins. Harper had

incredibly quick hands, which made him one of the

league's best defenders. After spending his first few NBA

seasons backing up Davis, he became a permanent part of

Dallas's starting lineup.

"Derek is always ready to play at the end of a basketball game,"

said Blackman. "He's willing to be a hero. He's willing to be a goat—

he doesn't care. You've got to get the basketball to guys like that."

In 1985–86, the Mavs continued to cement their standing as one

of the top teams in the Western Conference. While they were winning

on the court, however, they had problems in the locker room. Feuding

among Coach Motta, Aguirre, and three-point specialist Dale Ellis

JAMES DONALDSON

threatened to pull the team apart. Fortunately, Dallas made a midseason

trade for a player who would ease the tension: center James Donaldson.

At a massive 7-foot-2, Donaldson gave Dallas intimidating size and

strength in the middle. He also had an easygoing personality that

seemed to have a calming effect on the team. With Donaldson's

strength and character added to the lineup, the Mavs went 44–38 in

1985–86. Although they whipped the Utah Jazz in the first round of the playoffs, the Mavs once again fell to the Lakers in the second round.

Dallas was almost unbeatable on its home court in **1986–87**, going 35–6 there.

{TARPLEY LEADS TOWARD THE TOP} The Mavericks and their fans had grown accustomed to winning during the regular season. But they wanted to start winning playoff games, too. In 1986, Coach Motta engineered two key moves that he felt would carry the team to an NBA title. First, he drafted a towering forward named Roy Tarpley. Then he traded Dale Ellis—who had been unhappy in Dallas—to Seattle.

The moves paid off immediately. With Donaldson and Tarpley dominating the boards, Aguirre and Blackman scoring, and Harper guiding the team on both ends of the floor, the Mavs soared to a franchise-record 55–27 mark in 1986–87. Among those wins was Coach Motta's 800th pro coaching victory—the third-highest total in NBA history.

MARK AGUIRRE

The Mavs were confident that they would at last overtake the

Lakers in the playoffs, but first they had to get past the Seattle

SuperSonics, who were led by former teammate Dale Ellis. Ellis was out

for revenge against his old team, and he got it. Burying one long-range

shot after another, Ellis led the underdog Sonics to a three-games-to-one

series victory over Dallas.

Dejected after the loss, Dick Motta stepped down as coach. Dallas then hired former Phoenix coach John MacLeod to finish what Motta had begun. "The challenge for John is to chart new waters, especially in the playoffs," said Dallas general manager Norm Sonju.

Coach MacLeod did that more quickly than anyone expected. One of the best changes he implemented as coach was making Tarpley the team's sixth man. By coming off the bench late in the game, Tarpley often dominated his tired opponents. "With Roy on the floor, we talk NBA championship," said Blackman. "He brings us that little piece of magic . . . you see in a player who is superior to everyone he plays against."

In MacLeod's first season in Dallas, Tarpley and the Mavs cruised to a 53–29 record and playoff victories over Houston and Denver. They

Seven-foot forward Roy Tarpley helped carry the Mavs deep into the playoffs in **1988**.

ROY TARPLEY

With long arms and a soft shooting touch, Sam Perkins was a formidable scorer.

then moved on to the Western Conference Finals to once again take on

the Lakers. In a titanic battle, the two teams split the first six games.

Unfortunately, the more experienced Lakers took the

early lead in game seven and held on for the victory. Los

Angeles went on to win the league championship, while

Dallas again went home empty-handed.

{THE BIG CRASH} Despite the Mavericks' struggles

with the Lakers, Dallas fans were as enthusiastic as ever heading into the

1988–89 season. Their team had made the playoffs five straight years,

inching closer to the NBA championship every year. Tragically, all of the

Mavericks' progress was about to fall apart.

Dallas tore out to an early lead in the conference standings. Then,

in January, Tarpley was suspended for drug abuse. A month later,

Aguirre demanded to be traded and was dealt to Detroit for forward

ADRIAN DANTLEY

Adrian Dantley. But Dantley didn't want to leave Detroit and for several weeks refused to sign with Dallas. The team badly needed a big man, so it was forced to trade young forward Detlef Schrempf—a fan favorite—

to Indiana for Herb Williams. To top it all off, Donaldson went down with a serious knee injury.

In just a few weeks, the team chemistry that Dallas had worked so long to build was almost totally destroyed. Even though Dantley eventu-

ally signed and Tarpley returned from his suspension, the damage was

done. The Mavericks plummeted in the standings and

missed the playoffs.

Early in 1989–90, Dallas hired a new coach, Richie

Adubato. Adubato established a system in which each

player had a defined role: Blackman and Harper con-

trolled the ball and the offense, Perkins and Dantley chipped in on the

scoring, and Tarpley and Williams were expected to control the boards.

Adubato's new philosophy worked. The Mavs bounced back with a win-

ning record and a return to the playoffs.

But before the start of the next season, Dantley and Perkins left

town as free agents. Injuries to Tarpley also hurt the team, and the Mavs

fell to 28–54. Still, the Dallas faithful thought the bad season was a

Forward Rodney McCray hauled down almost eight rebounds a game in **1990–91**.

RODNEY McCRAY

Veteran forward Herb Williams protected the lane with his shot-blocking ability.

HERB WILLIAMS

fluke. They were sure that the team would make a comeback.

{THE "THREE J'S"} Over the next few years, Dallas fans

watched in agony as the Mavericks slid to the bottom of

the league standings. Rather than vying for the NBA

championship, the Mavs found themselves fighting des-

perately to avoid becoming the league's worst team. In

1992–93 and 1993–94, Dallas went 11–71 and 13–69.

Only late-season victories each year kept the Mavericks from setting a

new NBA record for the fewest wins in a season.

The only positive during this time was that the poor records con-

sistently gave Dallas top choices in the annual NBA Draft. The

Mavericks used these picks to rebuild with some of the nation's best

college players. From 1992 to 1994, the Mavs drafted three outstanding

young players: shooting guard Jim Jackson, forward Jamal Mashburn,

Guard Jim Jackson could either hit from the outside or muscle his way to the basket.

25

JIM JACKSON

and point guard Jason Kidd.

In 1994–95, Dallas suddenly surged to life with a 36–46 record.

The driving force behind this improvement was the Mavericks' "Three

J's"—Jim, Jamal, and Jason. Jackson and Mashburn combined to score

nearly 50 points a game, while Kidd dished out almost eight assists per

game and was named Co-Rookie of the Year.

Jackson and Mashburn were talented, but most fans considered

Kidd the brightest young star. At 6-foot-4 and 210 pounds, Kidd could

do it all: run the fast break, score, rebound, and shut

down opposing guards on the defensive end of the court.

Many basketball experts compared him to Lakers great

Magic Johnson. Even Chicago Bulls star Michael Jordan

once called Kidd "the future" of the NBA. In 1995–96,

Jason Kidd was a superb floor leader, handing out a whopping 25 assists in one game in **1995–96**.

Kidd backed up the hype, averaging 16 points and almost 10 assists per

game and playing in the All-Star Game.

On the surface, the talented young Mavericks seemed to be

heading toward a championship. Underneath, however, problems were

brewing. Mashburn was sidelined for most of the 1995–96 season with

a knee injury, and bickering between players began to pull the team

apart. The worst conflict was between Kidd and Jackson, who did not

JASON KIDD

speak to each other for much of the season despite playing side-by-side in the backcourt.

In **1996–97**, Shawn Bradley became the first Mavs player to lead the NBA in blocks.

The next year, Dallas featured a new coach, Jim Cleamons, and a new half-court offense. Kidd, who preferred to play in a faster-paced offense that allowed him to create in the open court, did not adapt well to the change. That, plus continued feuding among players,

28

triggered a major house-cleaning in Dallas. In a stunning series of mid-season moves, the Mavericks traded away Kidd, Mashburn, Jackson, and outstanding sixth man Chris Gatling.

{FINLEY AND THE FUTURE} When the smoke finally cleared from all the trading, Dallas had an almost entirely new team. Among the new faces in town were swingman Michael Finley, forward A.C. Green, point guard Robert Pack, and center Shawn Bradley. Although

SHAWN BRADLEY

this new lineup lacked the raw talent of the Mavericks' Three J's squad,

the attitude in the locker room was much improved, and Dallas was

eager to move on.

"We are very excited about this deal," Dallas general

manager Don Nelson said, "especially considering we are

acquiring Shawn Bradley and Robert Pack, who play the

two hardest positions to fill—center and point guard. We

feel the . . . trades give us a jumpstart in making the team competitive."

Guard Hubert Davis shot an amazing 49 percent from three-point range in **1999–00**.

The lanky, 7-foot-6 Bradley boosted the Mavericks' defense with

his great shot-blocking ability, and Pack gave the team steady guidance.

But Finley had the biggest impact. Over the next few seasons, the young

swingman consistently led the team in scoring with more than 20

points per game. Still, the Mavericks struggled. A 19–31 season in

1998–99 was the team's ninth straight losing campaign.

HUBERT DAVIS

Steve Nash assumed starting point guard duties for the Mavs in the late **'90s**.

STEVE NASH

Fans counted on high-scoring forward Dirk Nowitzki to make Dallas a force again.

DIRK NOWITZKI

The next season, Don Nelson moved to the bench as coach, and

Finley teamed up with 21-year-old forward Dirk Nowitzki to lead the

Guard Howard Eisley's tough defense helped Dallas rise in the standings in **2000–01**.

Mavericks to a solid 40–42 finish. A native of Germany,

the 7-foot Nowitzki proved to be a rising star with his

great agility and remarkable shooting touch. Dallas con-

tinued to strengthen its lineup by trading for forward

Juwan Howard in 2000–01.

After enjoying a successful run as one of the NBA's top teams in

the 1980s, the Mavericks endured much heartache in the 1990s. But the

team is determined to make a new start in the 21st century. Today's

Mavericks hope to break away from the competition and run all the way

to their first league championship.

HOWARD EISLEY